Top Ten Great Britons

Written by Jo Ne[...]

T0317894

Contents

Collins

What makes a great Briton?

The people in this book weren't born into greatness. They had to work hard and suffer at times for their achievements. Some benefited from a wealthy background, others from a supportive family, but they each had to forge their own path in a world of uncertainties.

Choosing the top ten

The ten Britons in this book were voted for by over 30,000 people living in Britain today, and range from people who died 400 years ago to those who only died in the last century. They include a writer and a musician, an **engineer** and a sailor, a queen and a campaigner, several scientists and several politicians.

All ten Britons were driven by a passion – something they were interested in or believed was worth fighting for. By following their passion, they went on to discover, invent and inspire – and create a lasting **legacy** that is still written about today! Aside from that, they appear to have little in common ... or do they? Let's meet them and see, starting with number ten.

10 Oliver Cromwell

1599–1658 • Born: Cambridgeshire

Who was he?

Oliver Cromwell was the son of a wealthy landowner. He studied at Cambridge University for a year, but returned home when his father died to look after his mother and seven sisters.

2000

1900

1800

1700

1600

1500

Cromwell speaking in Parliament

Cromwell married the daughter of a rich **merchant**, and together they had nine children. He made a living farming and collecting rent on his family's land. Later he became a Member of **Parliament**.

It wasn't until Oliver was in his forties that he played a much greater role on a larger stage.

In those days ...

There was great unrest in Britain during the 17th century. Charles I was king and he believed that everyone should obey him. In the 1640s, Parliament refused to raise money for the king and a war broke out. Oliver Cromwell was on Parliament's side.

5

What made Cromwell great?

Cromwell had no army training, but in the war against the king he became a successful **commander**. He chose good, honest men as soldiers, organised them well and won many important battles. In Parliament, he became a powerful voice too, criticising army generals and helping to form a new army.

In 1648, the king was defeated and Cromwell was one of the men who ordered his execution. Cromwell then became a leading force in the battles against the king's remaining supporters.

"He who stops being better stops being good."

Oliver Cromwell

Cromwell at the battle of Naseby, 1645

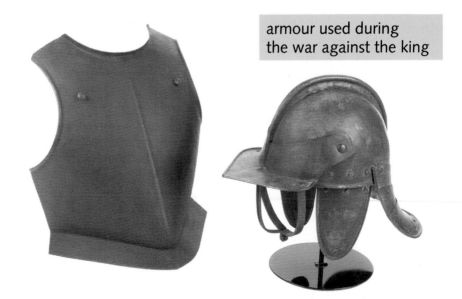

armour used during the war against the king

Once peace was finally restored, Cromwell himself was put in charge of running the country. He was given the title Lord Protector and he ruled for five years until his death.

Cromwell's legacy

Cromwell fought for a country where the king couldn't be the only person in charge. He made Parliament stronger and paved the way for modern politics.

Top fact

Cromwell had a grand funeral at Westminster Abbey. But three years later, Charles I's son ordered Cromwell's body to be dug up, hung and beheaded!

9 Horatio Nelson

1758–1805 • Born: Norfolk

Who was he?

Horatio Nelson was the son of a vicar and the sixth of 11 children. He was small and weak as a child, but his sea captain uncle inspired him to join the navy aged only 12. He became a captain himself when he was 20 and a commander at the age of 35.

2000

1900

1800

1700

1600

1500

Nelson married a young widow, Frances. They never had any children together, but Nelson later fell in love with Lady Emma Hamilton and they had a daughter named Horatia.

Lady Emma Hamilton

In those days ...

The British Royal Navy was the largest fleet in the world, keeping peace, fighting wars and protecting **trade routes** to Britain.

Nelson's flagship, HMS Victory

Top fact

Nelson suffered from seasickness all his life!

What made Nelson great?

Nelson was known for his bold decisions, his daring actions and his courage. He fought side by side with his sailors, sharing his plans with them and earning their respect. His many victories on the seas were reported back in England and made him a national hero.

Nelson lost his sight in his right eye during one battle and most of his right arm in another, but that didn't hold him back. Before one famous victory, Nelson put his telescope to his blind eye and claimed he couldn't see the signal to retreat!

the Battle of Trafalgar, 1805

At the Battle of Trafalgar, Nelson saved Britain from the threat of a French **invasion**, but was shot in action and died.

> "England expects that every man will do his duty."
>
> Horatio Nelson
> (spoken before his final battle)

Nelson is shot

Nelson's legacy

Nelson's **tactics** at sea had a lasting impact on the British Navy and his leadership style still provides inspiration today. Sir Winston Churchill even named his cat Nelson.

Nelson's statue in Trafalgar Square, London

John Lennon

1940–1980 • Born: Liverpool

Who was he?

John Lennon was born during the Second World War and was the son of a merchant sailor.
He moved in with his aunt and uncle when his parents separated, but his mother visited regularly and taught him to play the piano and banjo.

2000

1900

1800

1700

1600

1500

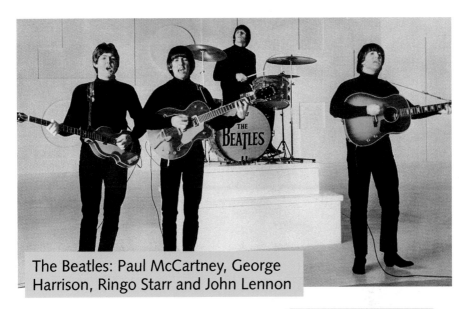

The Beatles: Paul McCartney, George Harrison, Ringo Starr and John Lennon

Lennon formed his first band aged 16 – a band that went on to become the Beatles and make him an international pop star!

He married twice, had two children, and moved to New York in his thirties.

Top fact

Lennon was thrown out of art school for being disruptive and failing his exams.

In those days ...

After years of war and recovery in Great Britain, there was a sense of freedom and hope. In the 1950s, an exciting new music style called rock 'n' roll developed. In the 1960s, cheap records meant more people could buy the latest music.

What made Lennon great?

John Lennon was a natural musician who had a witty, clever way with words. Together with another musical teenager, Paul McCartney, they became one of the world's most successful songwriting partnerships.

Lennon and McCartney's songs were upbeat and **innovative**, and the Beatles performed them with style and confidence. They became so popular, they had to hold concerts outdoors so that tens of thousands of fans could attend.

"My role in society, or any artist or poet's role, is to try and express what we all feel. Not to tell people how to feel."

John Lennon

cover of the album *Sgt. Pepper's Lonely Hearts Club Band*

In 1964, 73 million viewers worldwide watched the Beatles perform live on TV and 15 of their albums reached the top of the British charts. Lennon then developed a solo career, and three of his songs became number one hits.

Aged 40, Lennon was shot dead outside his home in New York, by a former Beatles fan.

Lennon's legacy

Lennon's songs introduced a new kind of sound that has had a lasting impact on pop music. The Beatles' albums are still bestsellers today.

The John Lennon memorial in New York is a mosaic featuring the title of one of his most famous songs.

Queen Elizabeth I

1533–1603 • Born: Greenwich

Who was she?

Elizabeth was the daughter of King Henry VIII and his second wife, Anne Boleyn. When Elizabeth was two, Henry had Anne beheaded. Then he married his third wife.

2000

1900

1800

1700

1600

1500

Elizabeth grew up with a series of **governesses** and tutors and became one of the most educated women of the time. Aged 25, she was crowned queen, following the deaths of her father, her younger half-brother Edward and her older half-sister Mary. She **reigned** for over 40 years.

Henry VIII

Edward

Mary

In those days ...

The country was very unsettled when Elizabeth came to the throne. She was the fifth ruler in 15 years, there was trouble between Catholics and Protestants, and England was at war with France.

Top fact

When Mary was queen, she didn't trust Elizabeth and had her imprisoned for almost a year!

What made Elizabeth great?

Elizabeth's reign brought welcome peace and **stability**. She ended the war with France, and her navy later prevented a war with Spain by defeating the Spanish Armada.

Elizabeth was a popular ruler, earning the nickname Good Queen Bess. She never married, which was very unusual for a queen or king. Instead, she said that England was her husband!

"I know I have the body of a weak and feeble woman, but I have the heart and stomach of a king, and a king of England too!"

Queen Elizabeth I

the Spanish Armada

Elizabeth sent sailors such as Sir Francis Drake to explore the world and invited musicians, poets and actors to perform in the royal court, including William Shakespeare.

Sir Francis Drake

Elizabeth's legacy

Creativity flourished under Elizabeth's reign and she was the inspiration for many poems and plays. Elizabethan writing, music and art are still being enjoyed over 400 years later.

Elizabethan dancing performed at Hampton Court today

19

6 Sir Isaac Newton

1643–1727 • Born: Lincolnshire

Who was he?

Sir Isaac Newton was the son of a farmer. His father died before his birth and his mother remarried. Newton was left to grow up with his grandparents.

2000
1900
1800
1700
1600
1500

The patterns of the world fascinated Newton, but he was hopeless at farming. His uncle suggested he should go to Cambridge University, and Newton later became Professor of Mathematics there. He also served as an **MP** and as Warden of the Royal Mint, where British coins were made.

In those days ...

In the 17th century, many people believed the planets, sun and stars moved around the Earth!

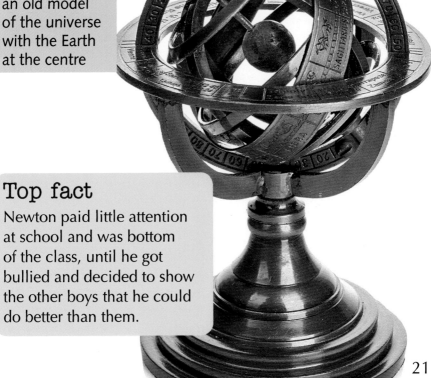

an old model of the universe with the Earth at the centre

Top fact

Newton paid little attention at school and was bottom of the class, until he got bullied and decided to show the other boys that he could do better than them.

What made Newton great?

Newton was the first person to realise that **gravity** is a force that happens across the whole universe. He developed laws about gravity and how things move, which explained why the Earth moves around the Sun.

Newton shared his ideas in a book in 1687. He was elected president of the most important group of scientists, the Royal Society, and he was **knighted** by the queen.

Newton experimenting with light. He discovered that white light is made up of a range of colours.

> "I seem to have been only like a boy playing on the sea-shore ... whilst the great ocean of truth lay all undiscovered before me."
>
> Sir Isaac Newton

Newton's legacy

Newton changed the way we see the universe, and his discoveries provided the basis for modern physics. His laws made space travel possible, while the new type of telescope he invented is still the main type in use today.

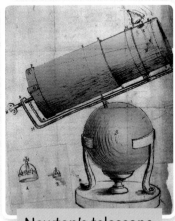

Newton's telescope

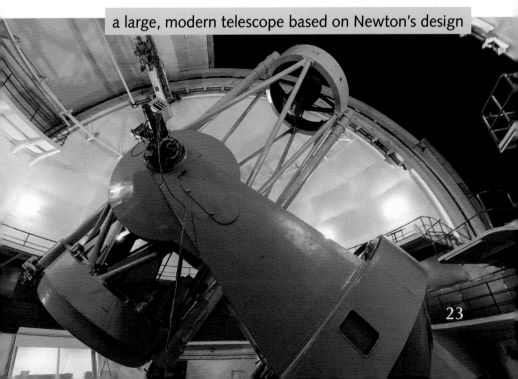

a large, modern telescope based on Newton's design

23

William Shakespeare

1564–1616 • Born: Stratford-upon-Avon

Who was he?

William Shakespeare was the son of a glove maker and the third of eight children. Aged 18, he married Anne Hathaway and together they had three children.

2000

1900

1800

1700

1600

1500

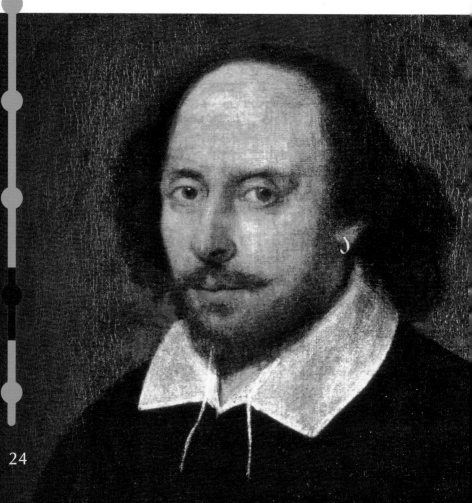

In his twenties, Shakespeare moved to London and worked as a writer and actor. He belonged to a successful acting group who built their own theatre, the Globe.

the Globe theatre

In those days ...

The late 16th century saw a huge demand for new plays. The first theatres since Roman times were being built in London. Stages tended to be bare, with just a few props and not much of a back-drop, so vivid words were needed in the scripts to describe the scenes.

a theatre performance in Shakespeare's time

What made Shakespeare great?

His plays! Theatregoers loved
Shakespeare's plays because
of the drama, excitement,
comedy, tragedy and
interesting characters he
brought to the stage.

a statue of Hamlet

"To be, or not to be,
that is the question"

from Shakespeare's
play, *Hamlet*

a scene from *As You Like It*, one of
Shakespeare's comedies

26

Shakespeare was motivated to keep writing really good plays because of competition from other playwrights and rival theatre companies. He also benefitted from having Elizabeth I and then James I as **patrons**. In total, he wrote at least 36 plays and over a hundred poems.

Shakespeare's legacy

Shakespeare's work has been translated into over 100 languages, turned into films and performed countless times over the last 400 years.

Top fact

Shakespeare invented hundreds of new words that we still use today, including: amazement, gossip, champion and moonbeam.

Audiences fill the rebuilt Globe theatre to watch performances of Shakespeare's plays today.

4 Charles Darwin

1809–1882 • Born: Shrewsbury

Who was he?

Darwin was the son of a doctor and the fifth of six children. As a child, he enjoyed walking, hunting, collecting natural objects and carrying out chemistry experiments in the garden shed with his brother.

2000

1900

1800

1700

1600

1500

He briefly studied Medicine at Edinburgh University, and then switched to Religion at Cambridge University, but his real passion was always nature.

Top fact
Darwin spent much of his time at Cambridge University collecting beetles.

Darwin's lucky break came in 1831 when he was invited to join the *HMS Beagle*, a British Royal Navy **survey** ship, on a five-year journey around the world. His role was to report on the wildlife in different continents.

HMS Beagle

In those days ...
Until the mid-19th century, no one really knew how different plants and animals came to exist. Darwin's own grandfather had written a book about the idea that one species could change into another, but it was hard to prove.

In 1839, Darwin married his cousin Emma and they had ten children. They lived in a country house outside London, where Darwin could concentrate on his research and writing.

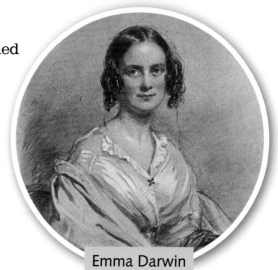

Emma Darwin

What made Darwin great?

Darwin's voyage gave him a unique overview of the natural world. He developed **theories** about how animals and plants adapt to different surroundings, and he collected many **specimens** to back up his ideas.

birds studied by Darwin in the Galapagos Islands

Darwin sent reports of his discoveries back to England and, by the time he returned home, he was a well-known scientist.

Darwin's real leap to fame came in 1859 when he published his conclusions on his research – the **groundbreaking** idea of **evolution**.

Darwin's legacy

Darwin's book *On the Origin of Species* changed our understanding of our place in the world forever.

"... from so simple a beginning endless forms most beautiful and most wonderful have been, and are being, evolved."

Charles Darwin

Top fact

Many people didn't like Darwin's suggestion that humans came from apes. Cartoons like this made fun of Darwin's ideas.

Princess Diana

1961–1997 • Born: Norfolk

Who was she?

Diana was the fourth child of Viscount and Viscountess Althorp. They lived on Queen Elizabeth II's estate in Sandringham, Norfolk. As a child, Diana played with the queen's younger sons, Prince Edward and Prince Andrew.

2000

1900

1800

1700

1600

1500

Princess Diana and Prince Charles after their wedding in 1981

Diana worked briefly as a nanny and a nursery teacher in London. In 1981, she married Prince Charles, the older brother of her childhood friends and the **heir** to the British throne.

The couple had two sons, the princes William and Harry. They separated in 1992 and divorced in 1996.

In those days ...

Before Diana married Prince Charles, the British Royal Family seemed very distant and out-of-touch with how everyday people lived their lives.

What made Diana great?

Diana brought a more approachable side to the **monarchy**, taking time to meet people, hear their stories and show that she cared about their needs. She was shy by nature, but her marriage to Prince Charles and her charity work at home and abroad made her a famous campaigner.

Diana talking to a landmine victim in Angola

Diana was president of Great Ormond Street Hospital for children.

Diana used her **high profile** to help others. She was the patron of around 100 different charities, and campaigned for many causes, including people affected by HIV/AIDS and landmines. She died in a car crash in Paris in 1997. Her funeral procession was six kilometres long.

Diana's legacy

Diana is remembered as the People's Princess. Her sons are now following in her footsteps, helping raise money and awareness for different charities.

"I don't go by the rule book. I lead from the heart, not the head."

Princess Diana

2 Isambard Kingdom Brunel

1806–1859 • Born: Portsmouth

2000

1900

1800

Who was he?

Isambard Brunel was the only son of a French engineer and his English wife. From an early age, Brunel's father taught him about shapes and **structures**. Brunel studied in England and France; then began work as an assistant on his father's project to build a tunnel under the River Thames in London.

1700

1600

1500

> "I am going to design ... a station after my own fancy; that is, with engineering roofs, etc."
>
> Isambard Kingdom Brunel

Bristol Temple Meads station

Five years later, Brunel became chief engineer on the Great Western Railway, linking London to Bristol. Many more major engineering jobs followed.

Brunel married Mary Horsley in 1836. They had three children and made their family home in London.

In those days ...

Britain in the 19th century was rapidly changing from a land of farms and small villages to a land of factories and big cities. There was huge demand for the newly invented steam train and over 9,000 kilometres of track were built in just 20 years.

What made Brunel great?

Brunel was one of the key engineers who made the railways possible by creating bridges, **viaducts**, tunnels and stations and planning thousands of kilometres of track. He was tireless in his work and found **ingenious** solutions to many problems along the way.

His groundbreaking designs included Maidenhead Railway Bridge, the widest brick arch bridge at the time, and Box Tunnel near Bath, the longest railway tunnel at the time. He also designed three steamships and a hospital for a war zone.

Brunel in his top hat next to the ship *Great Eastern* which he designed

workers digging a tunnel under the River Thames

Brunel's legacy

Brunel showed the world what engineers could achieve and he transformed Britain's transport routes. Many of his structures, such as the Royal Albert Bridge in Plymouth, England, are still in use today.

Top fact

While performing a conjuring trick for his children, Brunel accidentally inhaled a coin. He tried to remove it using a gadget he devised, but it didn't work. In the end, he had to be tipped upside down to knock it out of his windpipe!

Sir Winston Churchill

1874–1965 • Born: Oxfordshire

Who was he?

Sir Winston Churchill was the son of a politician and his American wife. He served in the army and worked as a war reporter before becoming a Member of Parliament.

Top fact

During the Boer War in South Africa, Churchill was captured and imprisoned. He escaped – and a WANTED poster for him was issued with a reward of 25 pounds!

2000
1900
1800
1700
1600
1500

In 1908, Churchill fell in love with Clementine. They married later that year and went on to have five children.

Churchill spent over 50 years in politics, taking key roles in both world wars, including becoming Prime Minister aged 65.

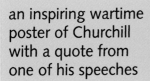

an inspiring wartime poster of Churchill with a quote from one of his speeches

In those days ...

After the horrors of the First World War, few people in Britain wanted to fight another war, but the threat from Germany under the rule of Hitler and his Nazi Party couldn't be ignored. In 1939, the Second World War began.

What made Churchill great?

Churchill's energy and **forceful**, charming personality helped him rise to top positions in government, including running the British navy and being in charge of the country's money. He didn't always make the right decisions and he wasn't always popular, but he had a strong sense of right and wrong, and he didn't give up.

"We shall fight on the beaches, we shall fight on the landing grounds, we shall fight in the fields and in the streets, we shall fight in the hills; we shall never surrender."

Sir Winston Churchill

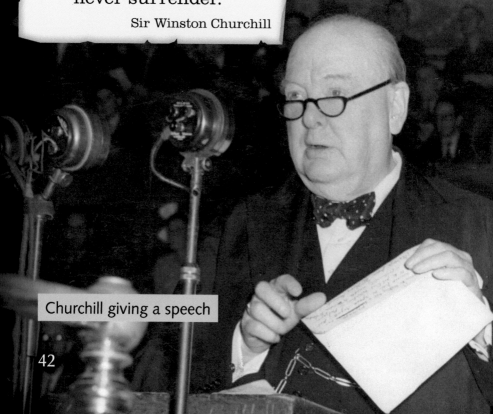

Churchill giving a speech

42

Princess Elizabeth, Queen Elizabeth, Churchill
and King George VI celebrating victory in 1945

Churchill's greatest achievement was leading Britain
to victory in the Second World War. Although he
wasn't the first choice for Prime Minister, he quickly
proved himself. His bold, brave leadership and powerful
speeches gave the nation courage to fight against
the odds – and win. In 1953, Churchill was awarded
the Nobel Prize for Literature for his writing about
the wars.

Churchill's legacy

If Churchill hadn't become Prime Minister in 1940,
it's very likely that Hitler would have invaded Britain
and the world we live in today would have been a very
different place.

Glossary

commander a person in charge of troops

engineer a designer of engines, machines or structures

evolution the way living things have developed

forceful strong and energetic

governesses women teachers who work in a private home, not a school

gravity a pulling force

groundbreaking never been done before

heir a person in line to take over a role when someone else dies

high profile attracting much attention

ingenious clever, original and inventive

innovative using new ideas

invasion the act of attacking and taking over other places or countries

knighted given the title of knight by the king or queen

legacy the lasting effect of a person or event

merchant a person who sells things in quantity

monarchy the crowned head and royal family of a country

MP Member of Parliament

Parliament elected people who make decisions for the country

patrons people who give money to support others

reigned ruled as king or queen

specimens examples of plants or animals used for study

stability a secure, safe position

structures buildings or objects made from several parts

survey carry out close examinations

tactics carefully planned actions and ideas

theories sets of ideas that can explain things

trade routes journeys taken by ships carrying things to sell

viaducts long bridges carrying a railway or road

Index

Great British characteristics

ingenious

courageous

caring

determined

imaginative

6

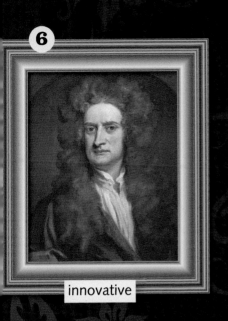

innovative

7

bold

8

creative

9

daring

10

organised

 Ideas for reading

Written by Clare Dowdall, PhD
Lecturer and Primary Literacy Consultant

Reading objectives:
- read books that are structured in different ways
- discuss understanding and explain the meaning of words in context
- identify main ideas drawn from more than one paragraph and summarise ideas

Spoken language objectives:
- participate in discussions, presentations, performances, role play, improvisations and debates

Curriculum links: History - British history

Resources: ICT, whiteboard and pens, paper and pencils, portrait painting materials.

Build a context for reading

- Look at the front cover together and read the blurb. Check that children understand what a "Briton" is in this context (a British person).
- Ask children to suggest who they think are "Great Britons".
- Turn to the contents and compare children's suggestions to the list. Practise reading the names correctly. Discuss what is known about any of the featured great Britons.

Understand and apply reading strategies

- Read pp2–3 to the children. Help children to match the names in the contents to the occupations listed, e.g. politicians, musicians and princesses.
- Discuss what a legacy is, and ask children for an example of a legacy. Check that the children can use the glossary to find the definition.